Noah's Ark

A Random House PICTUREBACK®

Noah's Ark

Illustrated by Charles E. Martin • Retold by Lawrence T. Lorimer

RANDOM HOUSE 🏠 NEW YORK

Copyright ©1978 by Random House, Inc. All rights reserved under International and Pan-American Copyright Conventions. Published in the United States by Random House, Inc., New York, and simultaneously in Canada by Random House of Canada Limited, Toronto.
Library of Congress Cataloging in Publication Data: Lorimer, Lawrence T. Noah's ark. SUMMARY: A retelling of the Bible story of Noah and the huge ark God asked him to build. 1. Noah's ark—Juvenile literature. [1. Noah's ark. 2. Bible stories—O.T.] I. Martin, Charles E. II. Title. BS658.L67 222´ .11´09505 77-92377 ISBN: 0-394-83697-9 (B.C.); 0-394-83861-0 (trade); 0-394-93861-5 (lib. bdg.)
Manufactured in the United States of America. A B C D E F G H I J 13 14 15 16 17 18 19 20

Once, a very long time ago, there lived a man called Noah. He and his wife and his sons and their wives all worked very hard. Now Noah was a good man and this pleased God. But all around him, Noah's neighbors were lying and fighting and cheating and stealing. This made God sad.

One day God spoke to Noah. "I am going to send a great flood to wash the world away," he said. "But I will save you because you are good."

At first Noah was frightened. How could God save him from the waters of a great flood?

Then God spoke to Noah again. He told him to build a ship called an ark. "The ark must be 450 feet long, 75 feet wide, and 45 feet high," he said, "big enough for you and your wife, your three sons, and their wives. Take with you also into the ark two of every living thing that creeps on the earth or flies in the air. Take a male and a female of every creature, large and small. Do as I say and you will be saved."

God told Noah many more things. Then Noah went home to tell his family all that God had said.

The very next morning Noah and his sons went to
the cypress forest to cut down the tallest trees for
timber. For many days they sawed and chopped.

Noah's wife and his sons' wives went to the fields to
gather fruit and grain and vegetables. They would need
plenty of food for themselves and the animals on the ark.

Soon the ark began to take shape. It was to have a wide, flat bottom and three decks—one for Noah and his family, and two for the animals. It would have a big door in the side and a window at the top. Noah's sons filled all the cracks with pitch, the black sticky tar that sailors use to keep water out of their boats.

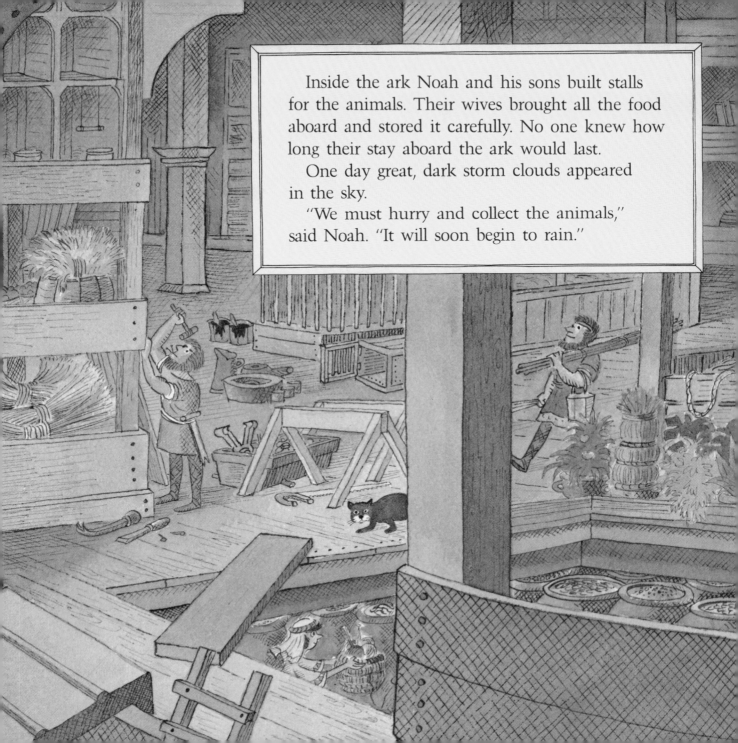

Inside the ark Noah and his sons built stalls for the animals. Their wives brought all the food aboard and stored it carefully. No one knew how long their stay aboard the ark would last.

One day great, dark storm clouds appeared in the sky.

"We must hurry and collect the animals," said Noah. "It will soon begin to rain."

So Noah and his wife and his sons and their wives went to the forests and fields and stables. They picked two of every kind of animal, a male and a female, large creatures and small.

They took snakes from their holes and spiders from their webs
and insects from their dark corners, and they carried them to the ark.
For even the smallest were to be saved.

Noah opened the door of the ark, and two by two the animals hurried in.

When all had been done as God had ordered, Noah closed the door.

Rain began to pour down. Creeks became rushing rivers. Rivers flowed into lakes. Lakes joined together to make a great ocean, and the ark was lifted off the land.

The great flood spread and the water kept rising. It covered fields and hills and mountains. The rain lasted forty days and forty nights, and water covered everything.

In all the world, nothing was left but Noah and his family and the animals on the ark.

The ark was noisy and crowded, and Noah and his family were kept very busy. They brought food and water to the animals. They swept the stalls and cleaned the cages.

Birds fluttered near the ceiling. Dogs barked and chickens squawked. Noah's sons spoke softly to the animals and told them to be patient.

Then one day, after 150 days of sailing, God remembered Noah. A calm breeze began to blow. All of a sudden the ark stopped floating. It had landed on a mountaintop.

When Noah opened the window he saw nothing but water all around him. So he let out a dove to see if it could find land.

But the dove returned to the ark exhausted. There was no dry land where it could rest.

Noah waited many more days. Then he sent out the dove again.

This time the dove flew back to Noah with a green olive branch in its beak. Somewhere there was a bit of dry land.

Noah waited many more days.
Slowly the water began to dry
up. When Noah sent out the dove
again, it did not come back to
the ark. It had found a place
to rest on dry land.

At last Noah opened the door of the ark and the animals began to leave. The sun was shining and the clouds were blowing away. The animals roared and mooed and trumpeted and crowed and chirped and chattered and squeaked. These were the first joyful sounds since the rain had started.

Two by two, the animals hurried into the world to find new places to live. Last of all, Noah and his wife and his sons and their wives came out of the ark onto dry land. The first thing they did was to thank God for saving them from the waters of the great flood.

On that day a beautiful rainbow appeared, and God spoke to Noah again. "God has sent that rainbow as a promise," said Noah. "He will never send another flood to wash the world away. From now on, whenever we see a rainbow in the sky, we will remember his promise."

Noah and his wife and his sons and their wives built new homes and planted fields. In time the earth was filled with people once again. And God was happy.